CW00551041

FOR BRIGHT LEGAL MINDS
WHO HAVE IT ALL

An Amusing Legal Book

"We've had tougher trials than this..."

Bruce Miller and Team Golfwell

FOR BRIGHT LEGAL MINDS WHO HAVE IT ALL - An Amusing Legal Book, Copyright © 2023, Bruce Miller. All rights are reserved for the collective work only. No part of this book may be reproduced or transmitted in any form or by any means, electronic or mechanical, including photocopying, recording, or by any information storage and retrieval system, without written permission from the author, except for brief quotations as would be used in a review.

This is book number twenty-one (21) in our *For People Who Have Everything* gift book series.

Cover by Queen Graphics. All images are from Creative Commons or Shutterstock

ISBN 9798862725605

The good lawyer. "The good lawyer is not the man who has an eye to every side and angle of contingency, and qualifies all his qualifications, but who throws himself on your part so heartily, that he can get you out of a scrape."

-- Ralph Waldo Emerson

What is a lawyer? "What are lawyers, really? To me, a lawyer is basically a person that knows the rules of the country. We're all throwing the dice, playing the game, moving our pieces around the board, but if there's a problem, the lawyer is the only person that has read the inside of the top of the box.

"I think one of the fun things for them is to say, 'objection.' 'Objection! Objection, Your Honor.' Objection, of course, is in effect saying, ''Fraid not.'

To which the judge can say two things, he can say, 'overruled' which is in effect saying, 'Fraid so,' or he could say, 'Sustained,' which is in effect saying 'Yeah, right.'"

— **Jerry Seinfeld**

Semantics. Two lawyers went into a restaurant, sat down at the bar, and ordered two drinks. As the bartender was serving them, they pulled sandwiches from their briefcases and started to eat.

The bartender couldn't believe it! He marched over and told them, "You've got your nerve! You can't eat your own sandwiches in my restaurant!"

The lawyers looked at each other, shrugged, and then exchanged sandwiches.

Can't get it out of my head. "A man won an $8,000 settlement from Disneyland after he got stuck on the "It's a Small World" amusement ride.

He said he'll use the money to cut out the part of his brain that won't stop playing the song."

— **Conan O'Brien.** TV host, comedian, writer, and producer.

Legalese. A judge in India wrote a mind-boggling decision. [1] It's baffling and very hard to figure out what was decided. Here are interesting and confusing excerpts of his decision,

"However, the learned counsel...cannot derive the fullest succour from the aforesaid acquiescence... given its sinew suffering partial dissipation from an imminent display occurring in the impugned pronouncement hereat where within unravelments are held qua the rendition recorded by the learned Rent Controller..."

"The summum bonum of the aforesaid discussion is that all the aforesaid material which existed before the learned Executing Court standing slighted besides their impact standing untenably undermined by him whereupon the ensuing sequel therefrom is of the learned Executing Court while pronouncing its impugned rendition overlooking the relevant and germane evidence besides its not appreciating its worth. Consequently, the order impugned suffers from a gross absurdity and perversity of misappreciation of material on record."

The Supreme Court sent the case back to the judge ordering him to rewrite it since it was "unintelligible". [2]

Other judges write more clearly. Justice Martin Sheehan of Covington, Kentucky learned that a long and involved case on his docket was finally settled. The case was fairly involved with tons of pleadings, motions, etc., and had been going on for years.

In his Order of Dismissal, he clearly stated the settlement was a relief and this "made this court happier than a tick on a fat dog because it is otherwise busier than a one-legged cat in a sandbox." [3]

The good judge didn't stop there, "Quite frankly, I would have rather jumped naked off of a 12-foot stepladder into a five-gallon bucket of porcupines than have presided over a two-week trial of the dispute herein.

A trial, which no doubt, would have made the jury more confused than a hungry baby in a topless bar and made the parties and their attorneys madder than mosquitoes in a mannequin factory." [4]

Judge Sheehan also asked the building superintendent to consult with structural engineers to make sure the building was sound enough to support the case file before it was returned to storage.

Trying to take the cleaner to the cleaners. Mr. Roy Pearson took a pair of pants to a local dry cleaner for alterations.

Sadly, the dry cleaner mistakenly sent the pants to the wrong location but corrected their mistake fairly quickly found the pants, and returned them.

Mr. Pearson, a lawyer, didn't agree that those trousers were his and sued the owners of the dry cleaner *pro se* for $67 million in damages.

The cleaners had posted signs "Satisfaction Guaranteed" and "Same Day Service" in their store.

Mr. Pearson argued the defendants did not honor and had no intention of honoring that purported unconditional guarantee of satisfaction to their customers, which he contends is an unfair trade practice under the Consumer Protection Procedures Act, D.C. Code § 28-3901 et seq. ("CPPA"). [5]

He claimed the "Satisfaction Guaranteed" sign rendered the defendants liable to him for seven different violations of the CPPA, for every day the cleaner was open for several years.

Pearson also sued for common law fraud based upon the "Satisfaction Guaranteed" sign and the "Same Day Service" sign. The trial judge calculated the damages and under the plaintiff's argument, and the damages could have been as much as the $67 million the plaintiff claimed.

The case went to trial and the judge held for the defendants.

Mr. Pearson appealed but the Appeals Court affirmed the trial judge's ruling that neither the "Satisfaction Guaranteed" and "Same Day Service" signs constituted false or misleading statements, or that they lost his trousers, and the trial court did not abuse its discretion in denying appellant's motions for a jury trial. [6]

What's next? A man asks his lawyer, 'If I give you $500, will you answer two questions for me?"

"Certainly!" said the lawyer. "What's your second question?"

Think you've had a long career? The world record for the longest legal career as a lawyer is 70 years 311 days (according to the Guinness Book of World Records).

The record was achieved by Louis W. Triay KC (1929 -2023) as verified in Gibraltar, on 1 December 2020. [7]

Louis was admitted to the Bar on January 26, 1950. He enjoyed sailing and was well liked throughout his life by many people.

He said, "The world is a stage – this applies to us lawyers. We need to know our lines and deliver these clearly and with confidence."

Courtroom Laughs!

Trial attorney: Now, in your report under the description of "Foundation" you indicated that there is a minimum of cracking and no signs of settling. Is that correct?

Witness: Yes.

Trial attorney: When you say there is a minimum of cracking, I take it that you did find some cracking.

Witness: No. There was no cracking. Because if I said there was no cracking, I would be in court just like this answering some stupid lawyer's questions. So, I put "minimum" in there to cover myself, because somebody is going to find a crack somewhere.

Judge: I could say I would like to shake your hand, but I won't.

Trial attorney: Move to strike —

Judge: No. We are not going to strike that.

Trial attorney: Move to strike the word "stupid," Your Honor.

Judge: The most appropriate word you want stricken? It is worth the whole trial.

Trial attorney: Do you recall approximately the time that you examined the body of Mr. Smith at your medical facility?

Doctor: It was the evening. The autopsy started at about 9:30 p.m.

Trial attorney: And Mr. Smith was dead at that time, is that correct?

Doctor: No, you dumb s#*t. He was sitting on the table wondering why I was doing an autopsy.

Trial attorney: "You seem to have more than the average share of intelligence for a man of your background," sneered the lawyer to the expert engineering witness on the stand.

Witness: "If I wasn't under oath, I'd return the compliment," replied the witness.

Finding a solution. "Well, I don't know as I want a lawyer to tell me what I cannot do. I hire him to tell how to do what I want to do."

– J. P. Morgan

You missed the big picture! Judge C. J. Callahan, a Federal appellate court judge, wrote a dissenting opinion using a well-known idiom.

"Concluding that this court lacks jurisdiction to review the denial of a request for an *ex parte* seizure order, the majority opinion accurately describes distinctions between familiar trees but fails to perceive the forest." [8]

Strange lawsuit in India. In 2019, a young man from Mumbai plans to file a suit against his parents for giving birth to him. [9]

Raphael Samuel believes that it is wrong to bring children into the world because "it was not my decision to be born."

He also plans to demand he be paid for the rest of his life because he was born without his consent.

On a Facebook page, he posted, "It's not that I'm unhappy in my life. I wish I was not born. My life is good, but I'd rather not be here."

His mother has a view on this too. Raphael told the BBC "Mum said she wished she had met me before I was born and that if she did, she definitely wouldn't have had me."

"She told me that she was quite young when she had me and that she didn't know she had another option. But that's what I'm trying to say - everyone has the option." [10]

He is still looking for a lawyer to take his case.

Logic test. State Supreme Court Judge Sam Smith's father has five sons who are lawyers. The names of the four sons are John,

Joseph, James, and Jordan respectively. What is the name of the fifth son?

Answer on p. 88

Finding a Lawyer. "Finding a good barber is like finding a good lawyer – you gotta go to the same guy."

– Ronny Chieng

Dismissed. A lawyer sued the airline in three separate suits for losing two pieces of his extremely valuable luggage and one carry-on briefcase. Unfortunately, he lost his cases.

Where are the girls? There are many lawsuits filed and usually, there are legal issues in most cases for the case to proceed further.

A frivolous lawsuit is a case that has no legal issues or basis in law or merit. There are usually sanctions or penalties imposed against a party who files a frivolous lawsuit.

For example, in 1993, Mr. Overton sued Anheuser-Busch for false advertising.

Some say Mr. Overton was overly creative in his thinking when he claimed he was misled by a TV commercial that showed a glamorous beachy site with lots of girls in bathing suits as long as you were drinking the beer.

He alleged in his suit that he drank a 6-pack of the brand's light beer but to his dismay, there were no visions of beautiful women on a sandy beach (as the advertisement he had seen seemed to portray).

He sought in excess of $10,000 in damages, claiming that the brewery used deceptive marketing and caused him emotional distress. The court threw the case out on the basis of a frivolous lawsuit. Mr. Overton appealed the dismissal of the case. It was affirmed on appeal.

Applying the law to the facts. "Law students are trained in the case method, and consequently to the lawyer everything in life looks like a case."

– Edward B. Packard, Jr.

What is a jury? "A jury consists of twelve persons chosen to decide who has the better lawyer."

   – Robert Frost

Thank you and wish I'd known you! Mr. Wellington R. Burt, a wealthy lumber baron (8th richest man in the US at the time) died in 1919. He was estranged from his family and friends.

He made provision in his will that his vast estate would be out of reach for his family until 21 years after the death of his last surviving children and grandchildren then living before the bulk of the fortune could go to his descendants.

His last living grandchild died in 1989 and 21 years later in 2010 his estate which had grown to around $100 million was finally distributed. [11]

First choice. "From the beginning, Mandela and Tambo were besieged with clients. We were not the only African lawyers in South Africa, but we were the only firm of African lawyers. For Africans, we were the firm of first choice and last resort."

   -- Nelson Mandela

How true. I find that when I tell lawyer jokes to a mixed audience, the lawyers don't think they're funny and the non-lawyers don't think they're jokes.

-- Chief Justice John G. Roberts, Jr.

Continuing in equality. "In the state of nature...all men are born equal, but they cannot continue in this equality. Society makes them lose it, and they recover it only by the protection of the law."

-- Baron de Montesquieu, French philosopher

An amazing man. Gerry Spence has never lost a criminal case before a jury either as a prosecutor or as a defense attorney. He has not lost a civil case since 1969. [12]

He's retired at the time of this writing (aged 94), and perhaps you might think he only took on easy cases. Some say anyone can win cases if the lawyer gets to choose the cases after determining it's slam dunk liability. Not Mr. Spence. He took on Karen Silkwood as a client.

He gained world attention for the Karen Silkwood case who was a chemical technician at the Kerr-McGee plutonium-production plant, where she became a vocal critic of plant safety, On November 13, 1974, she died in a one-car crash under suspicious circumstances after reportedly gathering evidence for her union.

Gerry represented Silkwood's father and children, who charged that Kerr-McGee was responsible for exposing Silkwood to dangerous levels of radiation and won a $10.5 million verdict for the family.

He had to take the case to the US Supreme Court which upheld the family's right to sue under state law for punitive damages from a federally regulated industry.

Mr. Spence and the Silkwood case achieved international fame and was the subject of many books, magazine and newspaper articles, and a major motion picture titled "Silkwood." [13]

When Gerry first started in 1952, he became a highly successful defense attorney for the insurance industry. But he left that after according to him he "saw the light" and committed himself to representing people instead of "big business."

He said, "Lawyers should be chosen because they can demonstrate a history rich in human traits, the ability to care, the courage to fight, the will to win, a concern for the human condition, a passion for justice and simple uncompromising honesty. These are the traits of the lawyer."

He seemed to fear nothing but there was one thing he did fear. "Nothing in the world is as fearsome as a bloody, battered opponent who will never surrender."

He had an interesting viewpoint on crime. "If you really want to stop crime, the best antidote for crime is justice. The irony we often fail to appreciate is that the more justice people enjoy, the fewer crimes they commit. Crime is the natural offspring of an unjust society."

And how does he view life? "That enigmatic trap called life: you don't know where you came from, and you don't know where you're going, and you can't get out alive."

Gerry Spence

Hard to stay silent. "Arguing with a lawyer is not the hardest thing in the world; not arguing is."

– **Raheel Farooq,** Pakistani writer and poet

Do you have a big workload? What is the secret to success according to Mark Twain?

"The secret of getting started is breaking your complex overwhelming tasks into small manageable tasks, and starting on the first one."

– Mark Twain

What a drag… Coshocton, Ohio is a small town (population around 11,000) and like any small town, they have immature young men disobeying laws. Two of those young men were Jason aged 23 and John aged 21, who happened to throw beer bottles at a woman in a car.

After being found guilty, Judge David Hostetler sentenced them this way. They could either,

- Serve 60 days in jail,

    or,

- Walk through the town for an hour wearing dresses, wigs, and makeup (to teach them respect for women).

They both opted for the dresses.

Let's meet - a riddle. Joe is the plaintiff's lawyer and agrees to meet with John, the defendant's lawyer, at a café to discuss a settlement at 2 pm. Joe thinks his watch is 25 minutes fast while in reality, it is 10 minutes slow.

John thinks his watch is 10 minutes slow, while in reality, it is 5 minutes fast. What will happen if they both aim to arrive precisely on time according to their watches?

Answer on p. 88

More semantics. A man in an interrogation room says, "I'm not saying a word without my lawyer present."

"You are the lawyer." said the policeman.

"Exactly, so where's my present?" replied the lawyer.

An equalizer. "Controversy equalizes fools and wise men in the same way - and the fools know it."

-- Oliver Wendell Holmes, Sr.

Lucky escape. Two armed robbers broke into "The Lawyers Club" an exclusive private club for lawyers. The lawyers and staff put up a tremendous fight and the two robbers staggered out ragged and beaten to a pulp.

"I told you we should've picked another place to rob!" groaned one of the robbers.

"It's okay, look I've come out with $1,000!" said the other robber flashing a roll of cash. "We'll split it!"

The first robber screamed, "Ass! What happened to the $10,000 you had from the job we did right before when we broke into this one?!!"

Safe refuge. "Lawyers are the first refuge of the incompetent."

   -- Aaron Allston

Actor. "In the courtroom, is where a lawyer really becomes an actor. There's a very fine line between delivering a monologue in a play and delivering a monologue to a jury. I've always felt that way - I've been in a lot of courtrooms. The best lawyers are really theatrical."

   -- Woody Harrelson, Actor

Unusual Motion. In the case of *William T. Moore vs. the State of Washington*, an inmate filed a civil rights violation action against the State.

The inmate was prone to filing numerous civil rights suits against the State of Washington, spending his time drafting unheard-of lawsuits and motions.

Seems he wanted to get more attention to his legal filings when he filed an unprecedented and exceptionally bold Motion with the Court calling it, *"Motion to Kiss My Ass"* in which his desired relief was to *"Kiss my God Damn Ass Sorry Mother F-er You."*

The Judge imposed a fine on the inmate.

An unusual will provision. Jack Benny was a successful radio, television, and film comedian. He learned to play the violin at an early age but was so bad at it, he used his terrible violin playing as his trademark. He passed away in 1974 with an unusual will provision.

He loved his wife Mary deeply and provided in his will that one red rose was to be delivered to his wife every day for the rest of her life.

His widow, Mary, didn't know of this will provision but found out after she kept getting one rose delivered every day since his passing.

Jack Benny

The most successful lawyer (so far). The Guinness Book of World Records reports that Sir Lionel Luckhoo who was the senior partner of Luckhoo and Luckhoo of Georgetown, Guyana, was successful in establishing a winning streak of 245 murder-charge acquittals in a row between 1940 and 1985. [14]

You might think he only took on small cases. However, this amazing world record was set when he acted as a criminal defense trial lawyer in 245 successive cases involving a murder.

In a few of the murder cases, juries found his client guilty, but those guilty cases were appealed, and all of them resulted in reversal and the defendant being acquitted. [15]

He also practiced as a barrister in England and later served as a judge of the Supreme Court of Guyana.

If you wonder how Sir Lionel Luckhoo did that, it's explained in a biography written by Fred Archer in 1980, and here is a brief excerpt,

"Sir Lionel would advise, 'Pick out two individuals on the jury. Look for one who is nodding his head and seems to be agreeing with you; then seek out another who is turning his head away because you do not convince him.

"Speak first to the one who is nodding. When you think you have won him over completely, move on to the one who appears dubious. Concentrate on him, look him in the eye make him feel that you are eschewing everything else to hold his attention because the life of your client is in his hands and that he must be convinced, as he ought to be convinced, that your man is innocent and deserves an acquittal."

Social laws Peter Principal etc.

Failures and advice. *Failures*: "There are two kinds of failures: those who thought and never did, and those who did and never thought."

"In a hierarchy every employee (including managers) tends to rise to his (or her) level of incompetence. In time every post tends to be occupied by an employee who is incompetent at carrying out its duties. Work is accomplished by those employees who have not yet reached their level of incompetence."

Advice: "If you can tell the difference between good advice and bad advice, you don't need advice."

"Some problems are so complex that you have to be highly intelligent and well informed just to be undecided about them."

"You don't need to take a person's advice to make him feel good, just ask him for it."

-: "Do it now. There may be a law against it tomorrow."

-- Dr. Lawrence J. Peter, Canadian educator and co-author of the Peter Principle.

Campbell's Law on planned social change. "The more any quantitative social indicator is used for social decision-making, the more subject it will be to corruption pressures and the more apt it will be to distort and corrupt the social processes it is intended to monitor."

-- Donald T. Campbell, psychologist

Pareto Principle. "Roughly 80% of consequences come from 20% of causes."

-- Joseph M. Juran. Engineer, consultant and author.

Murphy's Law. "Anything that can go wrong will go wrong, and at the worst possible time."

-- Edward A. Murphy Jr. Aerospace engineer.

No! No! Anything but that, Judge! Fort Lupton, Colorado is a small peaceful town yet there are a few who like to play their large car stereo very loudly.

Judge Paul Sacco has been known to sentence people who blast their car stereos too loud (violating town ordinances) to a taste of their own medicine by ordering them to listen to blaring music for an hour.

The music he orders them to listen to is not their favorite choice of hard rock. Instead, he orders them to listen to Barry Manilow, Dolly Parton, classical music, TV theme songs, and even nursery rhymes.

You might not have known this. You probably have heard of the famous McDonald's hot coffee case *Liebeck v. McDonald's Restaurants*. [16]

Many at first thought it was an entirely frivolous lawsuit since customers want their coffee hot.

Some of the alleged facts of this case weren't publicized as much as the initial filing of this somewhat unusual suit:

- The plaintiff, Stella Liebeck was a 79-year-old woman who suffered third-degree burns on her legs, lap, and groin.

- McDonald's had already received over 700 complaints about their scalding hot coffee but kept serving coffee over 20 to 40 degrees Fahrenheit higher than other restaurants.

- Liebeck sought to settle with McDonald's for $20,000 to cover her actual and anticipated expenses. Her past medical expenses were $10,500; her anticipated future medical expenses were approximately $2,500; and her daughter's loss of income was approximately $5,000 for a total of approximately $18,000.

- The jury awarded Stella $200,000 in compensatory damages, which was reduced by 20 percent (comparative negligence) to $160,000. She also was awarded $2.7 million in punitive damages. It was reported by media that the jurors arrived at this figure to penalize McDonald's for two days of coffee revenues, about $1.35 million per day. [17]

The main business of a lawyer. "The main business of a lawyer is to take the romance, the mystery, the irony, the ambiguity out of everything he touches."

    – Supreme Court Justice Antonin Scalia

Everyone else does. "Of course, I've got lawyers. They are like nuclear weapons, I've got em 'cause everyone else has."

    -- Danny DeVito, Actor

Duties. "Lawyers have their duties as citizens, but they also have special duties as lawyers. Their obligations go far deeper than earning a living as specialists in corporation or tax law. They have a continuing responsibility to uphold the fundamental principles of justice from which the law cannot depart."

    -- Robert Kennedy

Value. "There is but one thing of real value - to cultivate truth and justice, and to live without anger in the midst of lying and unjust men."

    -- Marcus Aurelius, Roman Emperor 162-180 AD.

Res Ipsa... "If the laws could speak for themselves, they would complain of the legal system."

— **E. F. L. Wood**, 1st Earl of Halifax

The Highest Court in the Land. Did you know that the top floor (5th floor) of the Supreme Court building houses a gym and a basketball court commonly known as "The Highest Court in the Land?

Supreme Court Justices, Byron White and Chief Justice William H. Rehnquist have been known to use the smaller-than-regulation court and Justice Sandra Day O'Connor used the gym for yoga sessions. It's not open to the public and can't be used when the court is in session.

A girl's best friend. I have learned that not diamonds but divorce lawyers are a girl's best friend.

-- **Zsa Zsa Gabor**

Get to know the people you want to be like. "I was one of the first women partners at my law firm, the first woman in my Minnesota prosecutor job, and the first woman elected from my state to the Senate. So, advice from women who had done similar things was important for me."

– **Amy Klobuchar,** politician and lawyer serving as the senior United States senator from Minnesota, a seat she has held since 2007.

Do you want to do this? "It's every lawyer's dream to help shape the law, not just react to it."

— **Alan Dershowitz**

No law and order. "At his best, man is the noblest of all animals -- but separated from law and justice he is the worst."

-- **Aristotle**

Pro bono. "I think lawyers who engage in pro bono service to protect those who cannot help themselves are truly the heroes and the heroines of the legal profession.

"As a child, I wanted to be a lawyer because I thought lawyers and the law were wonderful. But they are more wonderful, I think, than I had thought."

"I have been surrounded by some of the smartest, brightest, most caring lawyers, by agents who are willing to risk their lives for others, by support staff that are willing to work as hard as they can."

-- **Janet Reno,** lawyer and public official who served as the first female and 78th United States attorney general.

Janet Reno

Beginning Cross Examination. "How was your first marriage terminated?"

Witness: "By death."

"And by whose death was it terminated?"

Witness: "Guess."

Court persuasion. "Whoever tells the best story wins."

-- John Quincy Adams

Ugly baby case. When Jian Feng saw his newborn daughter for the first time, he was taken aback since the baby didn't look like him or his wife.

So, he accused his wife of cheating on him. His wife admitted she had several plastic surgery operations before they met.

So, Jian sued her for false pretenses alleging she misled him by hiding her medical background and the surgeries before he married her.

Jian won the case, and his wife was ordered to pay him more than $120,000. [18]

The nature of law. "In law, as in every other branch of knowledge, the truths given by induction tend to form the premises for new deductions.

"The lawyers and the judges of successive generations do not repeat for themselves the process of verification any more than most of us repeat the demonstrations of the truths of astronomy or physics."

-- Supreme Court Justice Benjamin N. Cardozo

What is litigation? "Litigation: A machine which you go into as a pig and come out of as a sausage."

-- Ambrose Bierce. Writer.

Fully armed. "Has he come armed, then?" she asked anxiously. "Has he brought a pistol or a sword?"

Ian shook his head, his dark hair lifting wildly in the wind. "Oh, no, Mam!" he said. "It's worse! He's brought his lawyer!"

— **Diana Gabaldon**, *excerpt from "Voyager" the third book in the Outlander series.*

Guinness World Record for the longest jury deliberation. The longest deliberation so far is four and a half months. In 1992 a case in Long Beach, California, it took a long time to even get to trial (11 years and 6 months). It involved Shirley and her son Jason McClure alleging that the Long Beach city officials violated the US Fair Housing Act by conspiring to prevent them from opening a chain of residential housing for Alzheimer's patients in an upscale neighborhood. The length of the jury deliberations took four and a half months. [19]

They awarded $20 million to Shirley and 2.5 million to her son. One juror reported saying "there was a lot involved." [20]

Good vs. Great. "Good lawyers win so-so lawsuits. Great lawyers can win lawsuits in which you have little or no chance to win."

-- **Dan Pena**, businessman.

Ever been mugged? During *voir dire*, the prosecutor asked a potential juror, "Have you ever been mugged?"

"No."

"Do you know the victim or the defendant?"

"No."

After a few more questions by the prosecuting attorney, the defense lawyer began in a friendly manner, "I see you are a teacher," he said. "What do you teach?"

"English and Theatre."

"Then I guess I better watch my grammar," he joked.

"No, you better watch your acting."

The potential witness was excused after the laughter ended.

Celebrities who attended law school. Some don't know many celebrities attended law school.

A few of them are British comedian John Cleese, Geraldo Rivera, Gerard Butler, Jerry Springer, Ozzie Nelson and others. Jeff Cohen (Goonies), and John Saviano (The Wonder Years).

Exercising the mind. "There is no better way of exercising the imagination than the study of law. No poet ever interpreted nature as freely as a lawyer interprets the truth."

　　　– Jean Giraudoux, French novelist.

Puzzling provision in Shakespeare's will. Not many know this. Shakespeare made a single provision in his will for his wife that she only be left the "second-best bed". [21]

33

Shakespeare had his solicitor specify in his will a provision that read,

"Item I gyve unto my wife my second-best bed with the furniture"

Although in those times, an excellent bed was a sign of wealth, it's still unclear to this day why he made this provision. [22]

Some historians argue his wife was already well provided for and this was just an inside joke between them. Others argue he might have been in an unhappy marriage.

A challenge. "Lost causes are the only ones worth fighting for."

-- Clarence Darrow

Plain talk. In *State v. Knowles*, [23] the judges on the Missouri Court of Appeals have been known to be a bit laid back now and then. This case involved a county in Missouri called Nodaway County named after the Nodaway River and is mostly agricultural with a total population of around 21,000

who are mostly country folk, one of whom allegedly was involved in receiving stolen property.

The trial court tossed it out as a criminal case. The appellate court didn't agree, and wrote this to tell y'all about it,

"Old Dave Baird, the prosecuting attorney up in Nodaway County, thought he had a case against Les Knowles for receiving stolen property, to wit, a chain saw, so he up and files on Les.

"Now Les was a bit impecunious, so the judge appointed him a lawyer, old Dan Radke, the public defender from down around St. Joe.

"Now, Dan, he looks at that old information and decides to pick a nit or two, so he tells the judge that the information old Dave filed against Les is no good .... Dan says Dave charged that Les "kept" the stolen chain saw and that's not against the law. You don't commit that crime by "keeping" the chain saw, says Dan; the law says you commit the crime of "receiving" if you "retain" the saw, and that's not what Dave charged Les with, and the judge should throw Dave out of court.

"And that's exactly what the judge did.

"But old Dave was not having any of that. No, sir! ...

"Bystanders could plainly see the fire in old Dave's eyes. He was not backing down. Sure. Dave could simply refile and start over with a new information by changing only one word. Strike 'kept'; insert 'retained'. But that is not the point. Dave knows he is right.

"And so he is.

"So, we'll just send the case back to Judge Kennish and tell the boys to get on with the prosecution." [24]

By the way, Nodaway County is known for horse trainers. It's the home of trainers Ben Jones and Jimmy Jones, whose horses won six Kentucky Derby races and two Triple Crowns.

Ironic. "Everyone wants to say they hate lawyers, and yet I've never met a parent who didn't want their kid to be a lawyer."

-- Jessi Klein, comedian and writer.

I'll be brief. "A lawyer is a person who writes a 10,000-word document and calls it a "brief."

– Franz Kafka

No bear wrestling. In 1996, the Alabama Legislature passed a law making it illegal to hold bear wrestling matches when it was held for profit.

The Alabama Legislature later repealed that law, but it is still illegal to be involved in bear wrestling based on anti-cruelty laws in Alabama.

Well trained. "I'm a soulless lawyer. Give me any opinion and I can argue it."

– **Megyn Kelly.** Journalist and media personality

A Poetic Case. The case of *Fisher v. Lowe*, [25] involved a suit where a property owner sued for damage to a tree on his property. The trial court held he couldn't claim damages under the Michigan no-fault insurance law and dismissed the case.

Judge J.H. Gillis wrote the appellate opinion,

"A wayward Chevy struck a tree

Whose owner sued defendants three.

He sued car's owner, driver too,

And insurer for what was due

For his oak tree that now may bear

A lasting need for tender care.

The Oakland County Circuit Court,

John N. O'Brien, J., set forth

The judgment that defendants sought.

And quickly an appeal was brought.

Court of Appeals, J.H. Gillis, J.,

Gave thought and then had this to say:

1) There is no liability

Since No-Fault grants immunity;

2) No jurisdiction can be found

Where process service is unsound;

And thus the judgment, as it's termed,

Is due to be, and is,

Affirmed."

After this summary, Judge Gillis wrote,

"We thought that we would never see

A suit to compensate a tree.

A suit whose claim in tort is prest

Upon a mangled tree's behest;

A tree whose battered trunk was prest

Against a Chevy's crumpled crest;

A tree that faces each new day

With bark and limb in disarray;

A tree that may forever bear

A lasting need for tender care.

Flora lovers though we three,

We must uphold the court's decree."

Questioning fees. "At the trial Stubbs chose to act as his own lawyer, but a conflict over his fee led to ill feelings."

— Woody Allen

Brainteaser. What will the time be? The clock below shows that it is 4 o'clock. If the clock is rotated 90 degrees counterclockwise, what time will it be?

Answer p. 88

The smoke ball case. In 1891, the UK was suffering from the tail end of the flu pandemic that was fatal to over a million people.

The Carbolic Smoke Balls company was advertised as a flu remedy and involved putting a rubber tube up your nose that was attached to a rubber ball at the end filled with carbolic acid. It would make your nose run and run.

The company advertised they would pay a hundred pounds to anyone who contracted the flu after using the Carbolic Smoke Ball. In today's money that would be worth around 16,000 pounds.

The company also went further in its promises and advertised it had deposited a thousand pounds with a bank to show its sincerity.

Mrs. Carlill tried the Carbolic Smoke Ball and used it regularly according to the instructions. She used the ball three times a day for two weeks and still contracted the flu.

When she requested a hundred pounds, the company didn't pay.

So, she took them to court and the court agreed with her and she won the case with the court declaring the ad was a valid contract with a bona fide offer, acceptance, and consideration.

Honest Abe. "Discourage litigation. Persuade your neighbors to compromise whenever you can. As a peacemaker the lawyer has superior opportunity of being a good man. There will still be business enough."

– Abraham Lincoln

Finding a solution. "We cannot solve our problems with the same thinking we used when we created them."

– Albert Einstein

Where have all the lawyers gone? In the old days (meaning in the mid-nineteenth century) 80% of the members of the US

Congress were lawyers. During current times only about 40% are lawyers.

There are more women in Congress than ever before. "Women make up more than a quarter (28%) of all members of the 118th Congress – the highest percentage in U.S. history and a considerable increase from where things stood even a decade ago," according to Pew Research. [26]

Ever been called for jury duty? If so, know that lawyers and law students are most likely excused since a lawyer or a law student on the jury tends to make the other jurors agree with their views.

In Massachusetts, a cat named Sal was summoned for jury duty because its owners had listed it in the U.S. census. [27]

Famous people have been called to jury duty. Even President Barack Obama was called for Cook County jury duty in Illinois in 2010. The Court excused him since he had to deliver the State of the Union address in front of Congress.

Over the years, there have been other celebs who served on juries such as Woody Allen, Marisa Tomei, Henry Kissinger, Calvin Klein, Robert De Niro, and Tom Wolfe.

Fighting over a cow. Two people were fighting over a cow. One was pulling the cow by the tail. The other was pulling on the horns. Underneath was a lawyer milking the cow.

You might have heard this one. A doctor, an architect, and an attorney were walking their dogs and the conversation turned to boasting about their pets. Each one had an exceptional dog and they decided to bet on who had the most intelligent dog.

The doctor was first and called out "Hippocrates, come!"

Hippocrates ran up to them and the good doctor told him to show the others what he could do.

Hippocrates ran to the park and dug into the ground and came back with a large number of bones. The dog placed them on the ground and assembled them into a complete, fully articulated human skeleton.

The physician patted Hippocrates on the head and gave him a cookie for his performance.

The architect shrugged and called for his dog, "Sliderule, come!"

Sliderule ran in, and the architect told him to show the others what he could do.

Sliderule immediately chewed the skeleton to rubble, then reassembled the fragments into a scale model of the Taj Mahal.

The architect patted his dog and gave him a cookie.

The attorney silently watched the other two dogs, and called out, "JD, come!"

JD ran up and the lawyer told him to show the others what he could do.

JD immediately auctioned the Taj Mahal replica to others in the park then left the auction proceeds with his owner less his usual commission.

First US woman lawyer. The first woman in the United States to pass the bar exam and become a lawyer was Arabella Mansfield who although was admitted to the bar and could practice law, she taught college and did activist work including work for Susan B. Anthony. [28]

It wasn't easy for her, and she had to file a suit against the State Bar of Iowa to take its bar exam. She successfully passed and was admitted to the Iowa Bar in 1869. [29]

Why are lawyers like pro wrestlers? "Lawyers are like professional wrestlers. They pretend to get mad and fight, but then they socialize after a trial is over."

     – Robert Whitlow, filmmaker and best-selling author of 15 legal thrillers.

The judge did not approve the settlement. A controversy arose on whether a Subway footlong sub was actually 12 inches around the year 2011. The question came up after an Australian measured one and posted it on Facebook showing it was only 11 inches and the photo went viral.

A class action was filed, and the parties reached a settlement 5 years later in 2016. [30]

During all this, Subway took measures to ensure the footlong was a foot long.

The settlement which awarded $520,000 to the plaintiffs' lawyers, plus $5,000 of "incentive" awards to 10 plaintiffs in the settlement had to be approved by Judge Diane Sykes who didn't approve it. She wrote in her decision not approving the settlement there was evidence that short sandwiches contained no less food by weight, and that uniformity in bread length is nearly impossible due to the natural variability of the bread-baking process. [31]

She wrote, "A class action that seeks only worthless benefits for the class and yields only fees for class counsel is no better than a racket and should be dismissed out of hand. That's an apt description of this case."

Comfortable. A lawyer is never entirely comfortable with a friendly divorce, any more than a good mortician wants to finish his job and then have the patient sit up on the table.

-- Jean Kerr. Author and playwright

The best lesson. An elderly farmer with a fairly large estate visited his country lawyer for a will. He told his lawyer he had only one son who never married and had no children. The farmer was a widower and had no plans to remarry.

The lawyer asked him about his son and the farmer told him of his son's alcoholism and gambling problems. He said his son didn't do much except drink most of the day and evening and play poker and added, "He doesn't listen to me."

"You need to have a trust. You could name your bank as trustee and give the trustee discretion to pay your son the income and principle of the trust. Otherwise, he could go to Vegas and gamble and drink away all of the money you worked hard for in your life."

"No, I don't want to do that, I want him to have it all when I die," said the farmer.

The lawyer tried to persuade the farmer to put his assets in a trust and even started to refuse doing a simple will for the farmer saying, "I don't want to get involved in doing a will for you. It's foolish for you to give your son everything where he could lose it all gambling. And I wouldn't look like I was helping you by doing a simple will where everything goes to your son. It will teach him how to value money."

The farmer thought a bit, then said, "If my son goes to Vegas and loses it all, that's the best lesson he could ever learn in his whole life."

An analysis. Truth or consistency? "The lawyer's truth is not Truth, but consistency to a consistent expediency."

– Henry David Thoreau

Surprise! It's your lucky day! A true story. Portuguese aristocrat Luis Carlos de Noronha Cabral da Camara was a loner who didn't have friends or any children. He left his large estate to 70 absolute strangers. He chose them randomly from a Lisbon phone directory.

Necessity of a Last Will. The Last Will(s) of Howard Hughes. More than 40 different wills were produced for Mr. Hughes. The most well-known was a handwritten will found on the desk of an official of the Church of Jesus Christ of Latter-day Saints in Salt Lake City, Utah called the "Mormon Will" [32]

The Mormon Will provided large amounts to various charities and $470 million to the upper management in Hughes's companies and to his aides. It provided that $156 million go to first cousin William Lummis, and $156 million was to be split equally between his two ex-wives Ella Rice and Jean Peters.

It also left $156 million to a gas station owner, Melvin Dummar, who said he found a disheveled and dirty man lying along U.S. Route 95, just 150 miles north of Las Vegas.

The man asked for a ride to Vegas. Melvin agreed and dropped the man off at the Sands Hotel. Marvin said the man told him that he was Hughes. Dummar later claimed that days after Hughes's death a "mysterious man" appeared at his gas station, leaving an envelope containing the will on his desk.

Dummar didn't know what to do so he left the will at a Mormon church office.

However, the Nevada court held the Mormon Will to be a forgery and ruled Hughes had died intestate – i.e., without a valid will. [33]

It took many years to settle his estate which involved a lot of litigation. His $2.5 billion estate was eventually split between 22 of his cousins.

Howard Hughes

Charge! "Lawyers are like rhinoceroses: thick skinned, short-sighted, and always ready to charge."

-- David Mellor

Oops! During proceedings in juvenile court, a teen was suspected of burglary. At the beginning of the session, the judge asked everyone to stand and state his or her name and role for the court reporter.

"Leah Rauch, deputy prosecutor," the prosecutor said.

"Linda Jones, probation officer."

"Sam Clark, public defender."

"John," said the teen who was on trial. "I'm the one who stole the truck."

Genius. "Everybody is a genius. But if you judge a fish by its ability to climb a tree it will live its whole life believing it is stupid."

-- Albert Einstein

You might have heard these.

- "What the big print giveth, the fine print taketh away."

- "Lawsome!" – means a fantastic legal person or legal event.

- "Excuse me, I am a lawyer. To save time, let's just assume I'm right every time."

- "If at first you don't succeed, try doing what your lawyer told you to do the first time."

- "Dance like no one is watching. Email like it may one day be read out loud in open court."

- "Justice or 'Just Ice' depends on which bar you are in."

- "I would like to request a brief recess, Your Honor since the witness's pants are on fire."

- "Happiness is being a lawyer and loving it."

- "Law is the only game where the best players sit on the bench."

Know this. "I think sports has done a disservice for a lot of black kids thinking they can only be successful through athletics and entertainment. I want them to know they can be doctors, lawyers, teachers, fireman, police officers, etc."

-- Charles Barkley

Charles Barkley

What exactly is the legal meaning of "golf"? Casey Martin, a professional golfer, had a medical condition that prevented him from walking long distances. The PGA turned him down when he requested to use a golf cart taking the position that would give him an advantage over the other non-riding golfers and walking the course was an integral part of the game.

The Supreme Court heard the case since it involved the application of the Americans With Disabilities Act.

Casey Martin won the case in a 7–2 decision. [34] The court found the PGA Tour should be viewed as a commercial enterprise in the entertainment industry for the economic benefit of its members rather than as a private club. [35]

The Court agreed with the Magistrate who heard the initial case who was Judge Thomas Coffin that the statutory definition of public accommodation included a "golf course", rejecting the Tour's argument that its competitions are only places of public accommodation in the areas open to spectators. [36]

The operator of a public accommodation could not, in Judge Coffin's view, create private enclaves within the facility "... and thus relegate the ADA to hop-scotch areas." The finding was originally upheld by the United States Court for the Ninth Circuit.

The intriguing and perhaps humorous part of this all was the dissent of Justice Antonin Scalia who wrote,

"We Justices must confront what is indeed an awesome responsibility. It has been rendered the solemn duty of the Supreme Court of the United States ... to decide What Is Golf.

"I am sure that the Framers of the Constitution ... fully expected that sooner or later the paths of golf and government, the law and the links, would once again cross, and that the judges of this august Court would someday have to wrestle with that age-old jurisprudential question, for which their years of study in the law have so well prepared them: Is someone riding around a golf course from shot to shot really a golfer?"

His dissent concluded by referencing Kurt Vonnegut's book "Harrison Bergeron." [37] If you haven't read it, Harrison Bergeron is a dystopian story taking place in the year 2081, where the 211th, 212th, and 213th amendments to the Constitution dictate that all Americans are fully equal and not allowed to be smarter, better-looking, or more physically able than anyone else. The Handicapper General's agents enforce the equality laws, forcing citizens to wear "handicaps". Handicaps were masks for those who were too beautiful, earpiece radios for the intelligent that broadcast loud noises meant to disrupt thoughts, and heavy weights for the strong or athletic.

Not friends. Whenever you put a man on the Supreme Court, he ceases to be your friend.

– Harry S. Truman

What is the record for the shortest jury deliberation? A. One minute. One wonders about this. In one minute, there may not have been enough time for the jury members to sit down at the table. Yet, on 22 July 2004, Nicholas Clive McAllister (New Zealand) was found not guilty of growing marijuana plants in Greymouth District Court, in New Zealand.

The jury left to consider the case at 3:28 p.m. and returned at 3.29 p.m. The defendant denied growing the plants and was found not guilty even though he could not explain why he ran and hid from the police.

According to the Guinness World Records one minute is the shortest on record. Apparently, the jury quickly decided there wasn't enough evidence for a guilty verdict. [38]

Admonishment from the bench. "In the future say 'I object' instead of 'that's total bullsh#t.'"

> **-- Anon.**

Exceptions. "The young man knows the rules, but the old man knows the exceptions."

> **-- Oliver Wendell Holmes, Sr.**

Large jury pool. The largest group of potential jurors in the United States was 9,000 persons called for the trial of James Holmes in Colorado who was accused of murdering 12 and injuring seventy in a 2012 attack at a movie theatre. [39]

The jury deliberated for over twelve hours and found Holmes guilty of the shootings on all twenty-four counts of first-degree murder, 140 counts of attempted first-degree murder, one count of possessing explosives, and a sentence enhancement of a crime of violence. [40]

Architect. "A lawyer without history or literature is a mechanic, a mere working mason; if he possesses some knowledge of these, he may venture to call himself an architect."

> **– Sir Walter Scott**

Research. "As the lawyer, I found most of it was a matter of research, which I was great at — that's what I did to death — and then basically persuading people that you're right, and they're wrong… I found that the easiest of all the professions to impersonate."

> **– Frank Abagnale.** Author and convicted felon and subject of feature film, "Catch Me If You Can."

Now that's a large jury panel! In Ancient Greece, jurors provided judgment on some court cases. The smallest recorded jury numbered 201, but usually, juries comprised 500 members. For important or controversial cases, as many as

2001 jurors deliberated and cases were decided by majority rule. [41]

Turned out fine. "During my first round of law school applications, I didn't even apply to Yale, Harvard, or Stanford - the mystical 'top three' schools. I didn't think I had a chance at those places. More important, I didn't think it mattered; all lawyers get good jobs, I assumed."

-- **Senator J. D. Vance.** Attended Ohio State University, graduating in 2009 with a Bachelor of Arts degree summa cum laude in political science and philosophy. While at Ohio State, he worked for Republican Ohio State Senator Bob Schuler. Then he attended Yale Law School, where he was an editor of the Yale Law Journal. Vance graduated from Yale in 2013.

Of course! A judge asked the young teen who stood before him why he broke into the Library after hours. "Tell me son, were you pursuing higher education?"

The young teen answered, "Free Wi-Fi."

Billable hours. "The billable hours is a classic case of restricted autonomy. I mean, you're working on - I mean, sometimes on these six-minute increments. So, you're not focused on doing a good job. You're focused on hitting your numbers.

"And that's one reason why lawyers generally are so unhappy. And I want a world of happy lawyers."

    -- Daniel H. Pink. Author of five New York Times bestselling books and a former Editor-in-chief of the Yale Law & Policy Review

In the hands of the jury. Many say jurors bring to court their life experience, common-sense, are expected (like judges) to act impartially, without sympathy, or prejudice.

Comedian Norm Crosby saw it differently when he said, "When you go into court you are putting your fate into the hands of twelve people who weren't smart enough to get out of jury duty."

No more juries. In 1960, three countries (India, Singapore, and South Africa) did away with the jury system. [42]

Where's my fur? "The mole rat is the only rodent born without a fur coat. With a good lawyer, someone would pay for that little oversight."

— Erma Bombeck

Judge riddle. Why would Snow White be a good judge?

Answer on p. 89

Don't mess with Mother Nature. The U.S. Supreme Court ordered a certain bridge across the Ohio River removed because it was an obstruction to navigation.

After the decision, Congress enacted new legislation declaring that the bridge company was authorized to maintain the bridge at its existing height.

Nature intervened and the bridge was destroyed by a storm. [43]

Foot in the mouth. A well-known car thief with a long history of car thefts was caught driving a stolen Mercedes Benz.

His lawyer who was known for his keen ability to sell a glass of water to a drowning man did his job brilliantly and got his client acquitted.

A few hours later, the lawyer's client (the car thief) burst into the trial Judge's chambers, with bailiffs right behind him trying to stop him.

"Your honor, just give me a second, please! I wanna get out a warrant for that scumbag, dirty lawyer of mine."

"Why?" asked the judge. "He won your acquittal. What do you want to have him arrested?"

"Well, your honor, I didn't have the money to pay his fee, so he took the Mercedes I stole."

Perspective. "When I despair, I remember that all through history the way of truth and love has always won. There have been tyrants and murderers and for a time they seem invincible, but in the end, they always fall... think of it, always."

-- Mahatma Gandhi

More Courtroom fun.

"Doctor, how many of your autopsies have you performed on dead people?"

Doctor: "All of them. The live ones put up too much of a fight."

Q. Doctor, did you say he was shot in the woods?

A. No, I said he was shot in the lower abdomen area.

Trial Attorney: Now sir, I'm sure you are an intelligent and honest man--

Witness: Thank you. If I weren't under oath, I'd return the compliment.

Judge asks a young witness, "Do you know what would happen to you if you told a lie?"

Witness: "Yes. I would go to hell."

Judge: "Is that all?"

Witness: "Isn't that enough?"

Q. Are you married?

A. No, sir. I am divorced.

Q. And what did your husband do before you were divorced?

A. Many things I didn't know about.

Q: Isn't it a fact that you have been running around with another woman?

A: Yes, it is, but you can't prove it!

Q: What did your sister die of?

A: You would have to ask her. I would be speculating if I told you.

Q. Are you pregnant now?

A. Yes. I'm two months pregnant.

Q. So the date of conception was approximately March 1st?

A. I guess that's correct.

Q. So, tell this court, what were you and your husband doing at that time?

Q. Did you know the decedent?

A. Yes. I knew him.

Q. Did you know him before or after he died?

Q. So, what happened then?

A. He told me, he says, "I am going to kill you because you saw my face. You can identify me."

Q. And, did he kill you?

A. ?

Q. And what did your husband do then?

A. He came home, and the next morning he was dead. That's all I know.

Q. So when he woke up the next morning, he was dead?

Q. Where you present when that picture of you was taken?

An old one. Trial attorney: Doctor, before you performed the autopsy, did you check for a pulse?

Doctor: No.

Trial attorney: Did you check for blood pressure?

Doctor: No.

Trial attorney: Did you check for breathing?

Doctor: No.

Trial attorney: So, then it is possible that the patient was alive when you began the autopsy?

Doctor: No.

Trial attorney: How can you be so sure, Doctor?

Doctor: Because his brain was sitting on my desk in a jar.

Trial attorney: I see, but could the patient have still been alive, nevertheless?

Doctor: Yes, it is possible that he could have been alive and practicing law.

The joke's on you! "The Washington State Supreme Court on Thursday announced a two-year suspension for a lawyer found having jailhouse sex with a triple murder defendant she was representing. Ha, Ha! Joke's on you dummies... I'm not really a lawyer!"

— **Tina Fey**, Comedian.

Can't decide. From the case of *Avista Mgmt., Inc. v. Wausau Underwriters Ins. Co.,*

"Motion is DENIED. Instead, the Court will fashion a new form of alternative dispute resolution, to wit: at 4:00 P.M. on Friday, June 30, 2006, counsel shall convene … on the front steps of the Sam M. Gibbons U.S. Courthouse …

"Each lawyer shall be entitled to be accompanied by one paralegal who shall act as an attendant and witness.

"At that time and location, counsel shall engage in one (1) game of 'rock, paper, scissors.'

"The winner of this engagement shall be entitled to select the location for the 30(b)(6) deposition to be held somewhere in Hillsborough County during the period July 11-12, 2006." [44]

Slum for the slumlord. Cleveland, Ohio is a fairly large city. Court proceedings were started against a man who owned about 40 slum apartments in terrible conditions. The Judge decided to teach the defendant the error of his ways and sentenced him to six months' house arrest in one of the worst apartments he owned. The defendant experienced exactly what his tenants had to deal with every day.

The judge also fined him $100,000.

Attack dog. "A lawyer is just like an attack dog, only without a conscience."

— **Tom Clancy**

Bad joke. "A pun does not commonly justify a blow in return. But if a blow were given for such cause, and death ensued, the jury would be judges both of the facts and of the pun, and might, if the latter were of an aggravated character, return a verdict of justifiable homicide."

-- **Oliver Wendell Holmes, Sr.**

The beginning of it all. Clarence Darrow was being hugged and hugged by a grateful client when he won the case.

"How can I ever thank you?" gushed a woman.

"My dear woman," Darrow replied, "ever since the Phoenicians invented money there has been only one answer to that question."

Clarence Darrow

Congressional observation. "Congress errs in too much talking, how can it be otherwise, in a body to which the people send one hundred and fifty lawyers, whose trade it is to question everything, yield nothing, and talk by the hour?"

-- **Thomas Jefferson.** American statesman, diplomat, lawyer, architect, philosopher, and Founding Father who served as the third president of the United States from 1801 to 1809.

When anarchy happens. "When anarchy is declared, the first thing we do, let's kill all the anarchists."

-- **Craig Reucassel,** Comedian

Non-justiciable issue or not. "It costs a lot to sue a magazine, and it's too bad that we don't have a system where the losing team has to pay the winning team's lawyers."

-- Carol Burnett

Best judicial systems around the world. The World Judicial Project is the world's leading source of original, independent rule of law data. Now covering 140 countries, in 2022, the Index surveyed more than 150,000 households and 3,600 legal practitioners and experts to determine how the rule of law is experienced and perceived around the world. [45]

The WJP Index is used by governments, multilateral organizations, donors, the private sector, and civil society organizations around the world to assess from time-to-time problems with courts.

The Index measures 44 rule of law indicators, or subfactors, which feed into scores for eight factors:

1. Constraints on Government Powers
2. Absence of Corruption
3. Open Government
4. Fundamental Rights
5. Order and Security
6. Regulatory Enforcement
7. Civil Justice
8. Criminal Justice.

Countries are assigned an overall rule of law score to each country.

In 2022, the top-ranked five countries with the best judicial system in the WJP Rule of Law Index were,

1. Denmark
2. Norway
3. Finland
4. Sweden
5. Netherlands

Ranks of other notable countries were,

- Germany 6th
- Canada 12th
- Australia 13th
- United Kingdom 15th
- United States 26th

The lowest three ranked countries were,

- Venezuela 140th
- Cambodia 139th
- Afghanistan 138th [46]

Looking for a good time? Painesville, Ohio, is about 25 miles north of Cleveland where three men were convicted of soliciting sex or, in other words, pimping.

Judge Michael Cicconetti ordered the men to take turns wearing a bright yellow chicken suit while carrying and displaying a large sign reading, "No Chicken Ranch in Painesville."

The nature of laws. "Laws are not masters but servants, and he rules them who obey them."

— Henry Ward Beecher

Tragedy. "The ultimate tragedy is not the oppression and cruelty by the bad people but the silence over that by the good people."

– Martin Luther King, Jr.

Look at that Mustang go! There is a law in Indiana that prohibits horse-powered travel to 10 mph. The law was passed in 1975 and you may wonder why that was.

Horses of course can run faster than 10 mph. The reason for this 1975 Indiana law was apparently due to people racing their horses which some say constitutes a public nuisance.

Observations from a criminal trial lawyer. Johnnie Cochran was born in Louisiana the son of an insurance salesman. He spoke plainly and to the point and was quite a salesman with well-known sayings like, "If it doesn't fit, you must acquit" or "If it doesn't make sense you must find for the defense".

He made other remarks that aren't so well-known such as these,

- "Money will determine whether the accused goes to prison or walks out of the courtroom a free man."

- "On January 10, 1963, I was sworn in as a lawyer, so next January 10, I will have practiced law for 40 years, and I've loved every minute of it."

- "Jurors want courtroom lawyers to have some compassion and be nice."

- "I'm a big believer in the fact that life is about preparation, preparation, preparation."

- "An opening statement is like a guide or a road map. It's a very delicate thing."

- "We've got to be judged by how we do in times of crisis."

Johnnie Cochrane

A funny lawyer. Actor Phil Morris, the son of actor Greg Morris (Greg Morris had major roles in the TV Series "Mission Impossible" as well as other TV Series) played lawyer Jackie Chiles in the Seinfeld series.

Many say his character was based on famous attorney Johnnie Cochran (even the initials were the same) and dealt with the legal side of unusual events happening in New York City in the series. Here are a few brief excerpts of some of his observations from the show,

- "You put the balm on? Who told you to put the balm on? I didn't tell you to put the balm on. Why'd you put the balm on? You haven't even been to see the doctor. If you're gonna put a balm on, let a doctor put a balm on."

- Jackie: "Did that warning label mention anything about damage to your appearance?"

  Kramer: "No, it didn't say anything."

  Jackie: "So you're a victim. Now your face is sallow, unattractive, disgusting."

  Kramer: "So Jackie, do you think we gotta a case?"

  Jackie: "Your face is my case."

Phil Morris

World record. What is the World Record for the largest payout in damages by a jury in a personal injury case to a person?

A. The Guinness World Records for the largest damages payout for personal injury to an individual occurred when a jury awarded US$163,882,660 to Shiyamala Thirunayagam, aged 27, in the Supreme Court of the State of New York on 27 July 1993. [47]

She was almost completely paralyzed after her car hit a truck that had broken down in the fast lane of one of the USA's busiest highways.

She agreed to accept a lower lump sum of US$8,230,000 and a guaranty that the defendants would pay up to $55,000,000 for future medical expenses. [48]

Serving. "What I seek to accomplish is simply to serve with my feeble capacity truth and justice, at the risk of pleasing no one."

-- Albert Einstein

Wise words. "How fortunate I was to be alive and a lawyer when, for the first time in United States history, it became possible to urge, successfully, before legislatures and courts, the equal-citizenship stature of women and men as a fundamental constitutional principle."

– Ruth Bader Ginsburg

Interesting view. "Actually, lowering the cost of insurance would be accomplished by such things as making it harder for lawyers to win frivolous lawsuits against insurance companies."

-- **Thomas Sowell,** American economist, author, and social commentator who is a senior fellow at the Hoover Institution.

Poetic Justice. In *United States v. Rosado,* [49] the judge responded to the defense counsel's rhyming request for a new trial.

"Counsel having had his say,

Anders, California

Would seem to say: "New trial, no way."

Forthright counsel I commend

For bringing this appeal to end.

"He has served his client well:

A worthless issue would not sell.

Dropping his quixotic quest

Serves his client's interests best.

"To press a cause of rank frivolity

Would not fill this court with jollity.

Though counsel was a courtroom terror,

He could not seed the case with error;

"So nothing now could be much grander

Than witnessing his posttrial candor.

Lawyers tend to look facetious,

Pressing issues merely specious.

"Frank candor sure beats false bravado,

Defending Claudio Rosado.

This is how I see the moral:

Instead of never-ending quarrel,

A broken record, crying "foul",

It's sometimes best to throw the towel.

"Thus, before the bar of court

This defendant must report.

He shall have to do his time,

For punishment must fit the crime."

And that will have to end this rhyme.

Anticipating. "As a lawyer, I can assure you that a lot of document drafting is repetitive, involving cutting and pasting from templates.

"But the best lawyers bring a unique perspective to the process and anticipate clients' problems."

   -- Ro Khanna

Creative sentencing. In 2011, a young couple, Grace and Nash, decided to raft through floodwaters in Geauga County, Ohio without life jackets. In the distance, a ranger spotted two people far in the distance without lifejackets rafting in the waters.

He took off searching and eventually located Grace and Nash and asked them if they had seen the two who were rafting without life jackets, which is highly dangerous. Grace and Nash lied to the ranger saying they hadn't neither seen them, nor did they own the empty raft that was found.

That caused authorities to immediately institute search and rescue teams searching the floodwaters. Many different government agencies had search teams out trying to find the two people the ranger spotted. The US Coast Guard even dispatched a search helicopter.

Still there, Grace and Nash were again asked a second time if they had seen the pair, but they denied it a second time.

Time passed and finally Grace and Nash admitted owning the raft on the third inquiry from officials.

Grace and Nash found themselves in court on first-degree misdemeanor charges facing possible jail time.

Well known for his creative sentencing to teach defendants a lesson, sentencing, Ohio Judge Michael A. Cicconetti showed mercy on the couple who sincerely apologized for all of what they put officials through. He gave them an option,

- Serve jail time, or

- Stand wearing life jackets in a kiddie pool handing out safety leaflets describing the necessity of wearing life jackets at a local event which had thousands of people attending for two hours and in addition doing 100 hours of community service.

They chose the second option.

What is the Guinness World Record for the longest trial?

A. Four years. In the case of *Frances E. Kemner et al. v. Monsanto Co.*, Case No. 80-L-970, heard in the 20th Circuit,

State of Illinois, the trial of the case took over 4 years with 600 trial days. [50] The case involved 22 consolidated actions brought against various defendants to recover damages for alleged injuries and property damage purportedly caused by exposure to chemicals released as a result of a railroad-tank-car derailment in Sturgeon, Missouri.

The Washington Post reported, Frances Kemner (age 81) said, "They had eight lawyers and we had two, but we licked them anyway." [51]

Living Trust result. An 88-year-old woman was called for jury duty and had to submit to questioning by the opposing lawyers.

"Have you ever dealt with an attorney?" asked the plaintiff's lawyer.

"Yes. I had an attorney write my living trust," she said.

"And how did that turn out?"

"I don't know. Ask me when I'm dead."

Disappointing sometimes. "The study of law can be disappointing at times, a matter of applying narrow rules and arcane procedure to an uncooperative reality; a sort of glorified accounting that serves to regulate the affairs of those who have power—and that all too often seeks to explain, to those who do not, the ultimate wisdom and justness of their condition.

"But that's not all the law is. The law is also memory; the law also records a long-running conversation, a nation arguing with its conscience."

– **Barack Obama** excerpt from "Dreams from My Father: A Story of Race and Inheritance"

Eventually. A new young lawyer had just been hired by a small firm. He struggled hard and passed the bar exam on his fourth try.

He worked hard at his new job. He prepared and dictated court pleadings and handed them to his new secretary to transcribe.

She came back after working on the pleadings and pointed out there was a small error below the signature line after his name which should have read "Attorney at Law".

The young lawyer saw the error and said, "Must you rub it in?"

He had dictated "Attorney at Last."

The complexity and depth of the legal system. "The end of law is not to abolish or restrain, but to preserve and enlarge freedom. For in all the states of created beings capable of law, where there is no law, there is no freedom." – **John Locke**

"Law and order are the medicine of the body politic and when the body politic gets sick, medicine must be administered." -- **B.R. Ambedkar**

"I submit that an individual who breaks a law that conscience tells him is unjust, and who willingly accepts the penalty of imprisonment in order to arouse the conscience of the community over its injustice, is in reality expressing the highest respect for law." **-- Martin Luther King Jr.**

A word of thanks. "Some say lawyers are brilliant people with exceptionally good analytical, research and people skills. Lawyers are often subjected to stress, long hours, and complex cases and clients. Lawyers are one of the most fascinating group of men and women anyone wants to get to know better and have as neighbors." -- Anon.

Most active bar memberships. You might have lawyer Michael Sauer as a neighbor since according to the Guinness Book of World Records, Michael has been admitted to practice in 47 states (a world record). This record was recently set on August 10, 2023.

Guinness reports Michael wants to demonstrate his commitment and pursuit of being able to provide legal representation in jurisdictions across the country. He wants to inspire other individuals to follow in his footsteps and pursue their goals. [52]

Question. "If lawyers are disbarred and clergymen defrocked, doesn't it follow that electricians can be delighted, musicians denoted, cowboys deranged, models deposed, tree surgeons debarked, and dry cleaners depressed?"

— Steven Wright

Special vision. "Lawyers have a way of seeing that sets them apart from the rest of us. In some ways this special vision makes them invaluable, and in other ways, repulsive.

"Lawyers are much more focused on rational, logical, and objective criteria to the exclusion of the emotional, subjective, and sometimes irrational responses to the world.

"Moreover, lawyers like to show no emotion, and possess a particular disdain for the emotions that are found in others, which has the quality of making them seem inhuman."

— Thane Rosenbaum, Writer and novelist.

Why did that chicken cross the road? In Quitman, George, you've got to watch your chickens! Chickens are protected under specific transport safety laws.

Part II, Chapter 8 Animals and Fowls provides, "It shall be unlawful for any person owning or controlling chickens, ducks, geese or any other domestic fowl to allow the same to run at large upon the streets or alleys of the city or to be upon the premises of any other person, without the consent of such other person." [53]

Maturity in court pleadings. In the US District Court for the Southern District of Texas case of *Bradshaw v. Unity Marine* the District Judge Samuel Kent wrote an order granting summary judgment in a personal injury case in the Plaintiff's favor. [54]

His order is interesting to read and here are brief excerpts,

"Take heed and be suitably awed, oh boys and girls - the Court was able to state the issue and its resolution in one paragraph ... despite dozens of pages of gibberish from the parties to the contrary!"

Judge Kent also noted this case involved the most "amateurish pleadings" he'd ever seen. It's worth a read.

He also wrote in the Order,

- "Before proceeding further, the Court notes that this case involves two extremely likable lawyers, who have together delivered some of the most amateurish pleadings ever to cross the hallowed causeway into Galveston, an effort which leads the Court to surmise but one plausible explanation.

- "Both attorneys have obviously entered into a secret pact complete with hats, handshakes and cryptic words to draft their pleadings entirely in crayon on the back sides of gravy-stained paper placemats, in the hope that the Court would be so charmed by their child-like efforts that their utter dearth of legal authorities in their briefing would go unnoticed.

- "Whatever actually occurred, the Court is now faced with the daunting task of deciphering their submissions. With Big Chief tablet readied, thick black pencil in hand, and a devil-may-care laugh in the face of death, life on the razor's edge sense of exhilaration, the Court begins.

- "At this juncture, Plaintiff retains, albeit seemingly to his befuddlement and/or consternation, a maritime law cause of action versus his alleged Jones Act employer, Defendant Unity Marine Corporation, Inc.

- "However, it is well known around these parts that Unity Marine's lawyer is equally likable and has been writing crisply in ink since the second grade. Some old-timers even spin yarns of an ability to type.

- "The Court cannot speak to the veracity of such loose talk, but out of caution, the Court suggests that Plaintiff's lovable counsel had best upgrade to a nice shiny No. 2 pencil or at least sharpen what's left of the stubs of his crayons for what remains of this heart-stopping, spine-tingling action. The court noted that "In either case, the Court cautions Plaintiff's counsel not to run with a sharpened writing utensil in hand he could put his eye out." [55]

Rules. "You are remembered for the rules you break."

-- General Douglas MacArthur

Persuasion. "Only lawyers and painters can turn white to black." **-- Japanese Proverb**

Why are you leaving your money to the dogs? Billionaire Leona Helmsley had an estate of approximately $4 billion and provided that $12 million of her estate was to be held for the care of her dogs.

Her dog was named "Trouble" and $12 million was put in trust to care for this Maltese dog.

She left a share for her 4 grandchildren provided they would visit their father's grave annually to inherit their share as she provided.

She left more funds in a charitable trust as well for the care of animals.

A judge reduced 8-year-old Trouble's share to $2 million. Sadly, there were plenty of anonymous death and kidnap threats.

Some say it's not a good idea to leave your money to the dogs.

Others say that when the relatives leave after the burial, it's only the dog that sleeps on the grave.

Leadership. The challenge of leadership is to be strong, but not rude; be kind, but not weak; be bold, but not bully; be thoughtful, but not lazy; be humble, but not timid; be proud, but not arrogant; have humor, but without folly.

– Jim Rohn

Synonyms. "What's another word for Thesaurus?

-- Stephen Wright

(Love the pun! See the serious answer p. 89.)

Harper Lee, "To Kill a Mockingbird" Atticus Finch battling away.

- "You just hold your head high and keep those fists down. No matter what anybody says to you, don't you let 'em get your goat. Try fighting with your head for a change."

- "Simply because we were licked a hundred years before we started is no reason for us not to try to win."

- "I wanted you to see what real courage is, instead of getting the idea that courage is a man with a gun in his hand. It's when you know you're licked before you begin but you begin anyway, and you see it through no matter what. You rarely win, but sometimes you do."

Answers to Riddles

Q. Judge Sam Smith's father has five sons who are lawyers. The names of the four sons are John, Joseph, James, and Jordan respectively. What is the name of the fifth son?

A. Sam. The judge's father has four sons and four of them have been named. Of course, the fifth son is the Judge himself.

Let's meet riddle. Joe the plaintiff's lawyer agrees to meet with John the defendant's lawyer at a café to discuss a settlement at 2 p.m. Joe thinks his watch is 25 minutes fast while in reality it is 10 minutes slow.

John thinks his watch is 10 minutes slow, while in reality it is 5 minutes fast. What will happen if they both aim to arrive precisely on time according to their watches?

A. Joe will be 35 minutes late. John will arrive at 1:45 p.m., 15 minutes ahead of time.

Brainteaser. What will the time be? The clock below shows that it is 4 o'clock. If the clock is rotated 90 degrees counterclockwise, what time will it be?

A. 12:45. The obvious trick in this riddle is the word counterclockwise. A majority of people seem to seem to get this by turning the clock clockwise.

Judge riddle. Why would Snow White be a good judge?

A. Because she's the fairest in the land.

Synonyms. "What's another word for Thesaurus?"

Another name for Thesaurus is onomasticon.

We hope you enjoyed the book!

If you liked the book, we would sincerely appreciate your taking a few moments to leave a brief review.

Thank you again very much!

Bruce Miller

bruce@teamgolfwell.com

Other Books by Bruce Miller and Team Golfwell

Books in our "For People Who Have Everything Series (21 Books)"

For the Greatest Cook Who Has It All!

For the Golfer Who Has Everything: A Funny Golf Book

For a Great Fisherman Who Has Everything: A Funny Book for Fishermen

For a Tennis Player Who Has Everything: A Funny Tennis Book

For Wonderful & Clever Kids Who Love to Laugh!

The Funniest Quotations to Brighten Every Day: Brilliant, Inspiring, and Hilarious Thoughts from Great Minds

Jokes for Very Funny Kids (Big & Little): Funny Jokes and Riddles Ages 9 - 12 and up and many more.

And many more…

Index

References

[1] In the High Court of Himachal Pradesh Shimlac.R. No. 184 of 2011.Reserved on: 24.11.2016. Decided on: 5th December 2016

[2] Ibid.

[3] Kisel v. Schwartz & Maines & Ruby Co., Case No. 09-CI-00165, Kenton Circuit Ct., Ky, Jul. 19, 2011.

[4] Ibid.

[5] Pearson v. Chung , 05 CA 4302 (D.C. Sup. Ct. 2007)

[6] Ibid.

[7] Longest Legal Career, Guinness World Records, https://www.guinnessworldrecords.com/world-records/longest-career-as-a-lawyer

[8] (In re Lorillard Tobacco Co., 370 F.3d 982, 991 (9th Cir. 2004) (Callahan, C. J., dissenting).)

[9] Weird court cases filed, Dailyo.in, https://www.dailyo.in/variety/weird-court-cases-filed-35899

[10] Ibid.

[11] Wellington R. Burt, Wikipedia, https://en.wikipedia.org/wiki/Wellington_R._Burt

[12] Gerry Spence, Wikipedia, https://en.wikipedia.org/wiki/Gerry_Spence

[13] Ibid.

[14] World's most successful lawyer, Guinness World Records, https://www.guinnessworldrecords.com/world-records/most-successful-lawyer/

[15] Lionell Luckhoo, Wikipedia, https://en.wikipedia.org/wiki/Lionel_Luckhoo

[16] Liebeck v. McDonalds Restaurants, Wikipedia, https://en.wikipedia.org/wiki/Liebeck_v._McDonald%27s_Restaurants

[17] Ibid.

[18] Chinese man sues wife, Daily Mail, https://www.dailymail.co.uk/news/article-2223718/Chinese-man-sues-wife-ugly-court-AGREES--awarding-120-000.html

[19] Longest Jury Deliberation, Guinness World Records, https://www.guinnessworldrecords.com/world-records/93247-longest-jury-deliberation

[20] Cases in the news, https://kkcomcon.com/doc/McClure-v-Long-Beach.P1.pdf

[21] What was the second-best bed? Shakespeare.org., https://www.shakespeare.org.uk/explore-shakespeare/shakespedia/william-shakespeare/second-best-bed/

[22] Ibid.

[23] State v. Knowles, 739 S.W.2d 753, 754 (Mo. Ct. App. 1987)

[24] Ibid.

[25] Fisher v. Lowe, 122 Mich. App. 418

[26] Women make up a record number of the 118th Congress, Pew Research, https://www.pewresearch.org/short-reads/2023/01/03/118th-congress-has-a-record-number-of-women/

[27] A cat in Boston was summonsed for jury duty, OMG facts, http://www.omgfacts.com/lists/5496/A-cat-in-Boston-was-summoned-for-jury-duty-ab572-0)

[28] Arabella Mansfield, Wikipedia, https://en.wikipedia.org/wiki/Arabella_Mansfieldhttps://en.wikipedia.org/wiki/Arabella_Mansfield

[29] Ibid.

[30] In re: Subway Footlong Sandwich Marketing and Sales Practices Litigation, 7th U.S. Circuit Court of Appeals, No. 16-1652

[31] Ibid.

[32] Howard Hughes, Wikipedia, https://en.wikipedia.org/wiki/Howard_Hughes

[33] Ibid.

[34] PGA Tour, Inc. v. Martin, 532 U.S. 661 (2001)

[35] PGA Tour v. Martin, Wikipedia, https://en.wikipedia.org/wiki/PGA_Tour,_Inc._v._Martin

[36] Ibid.

[37] Ibid.

[38] Shortest Jury Deliberation, Guinness World Records, https://www.guinnessworldrecords.com/world-records/shortest-jury-deliberation

[39] Mangan, F., Burke, K.D., & Acuna, A. (20 January 2015) Largest jury pool in US history gathered as Colo., http://www.foxnews.com/us/2015/01/20/jury-selection-to-begin-in-colorado-theater-shooting-trial/

[40] James Holmes, Wikipedia, https://en.wikipedia.org/wiki/James_Holmes_(mass_murderer)

[41] (Mueller, J., (n.d.) The jury in a court of law in Ancient Greece. http://classroom.synonym.com/jury-court-law-ancient-greece-12337.html)

[42] Vander Hook, S., (2011) Democracy. Minnesota: ABDO Publishing Company

[43] (Pennsylvania v. Wheeling & Belmont Bridge Co., 54 U.S. (13 How.) 518 (1852).)

[44] Avista Mgmt., Inc. v. Wausau Underwriters Ins. Co., No. 6:05-CV1430ORL31JGG, 2006 WL 1562246, (M.D. Fla. June 6, 2006).

[45] World Justice Project News, Rule of Law Index, https://worldjusticeproject.org/news/wjp-rule-law-index-2022-global-press-release

[46] Ibid.

[47] Greatest payout for personal injury damages to an individual, Guinness World Records, http://www.guinnessworldrecords.com/world-records/greatest-payout-for-personal-injurydamages-to-an-individual)

[48] Ibid.

[49] United States v. Rosado, No. CIV.A.90-00457, 1991 WL 59608 (E.D. Pa. April 12, 1991)

[50] Frances E. Kemner et al. v. Monsanto Co., Case No. 80-L-970, heard in the 20th Circuit, State of Illinois

[51] The Little Town that Whipped Monsanto, Washington Post, https://www.washingtonpost.com/archive/lifestyle/1987/11/08/the-little-town-that-whipped-monsanto/eaa0d5c0-c941-4a85-b960-5ac97cb76406/

[52] Most Active Bar Memberships, Guinness World Records, https://www.guinnessworldrecords.com/world-records/78787-most-active-bar-memberships-for-an-attorney

[53] Municode.com, https://library.municode.com/ga/quitman/codes/code_of_ordinances?nodeId=PTIICOOR_CH8ANFO

[54] Bradshaw v. Unity Marine Corp., Inc., 147 F. Supp. 2d 668 (S.D. Tex. 2001)

[55] Ibid.

Printed in Great Britain
by Amazon

35470522R00061